SANDY KOUFAX

by
William R. Sanford
&
Carl R. Green

New York

Maxwell Macmillan Canada
Toronto

Maxwell Macmillan International
New York Oxford Singapore Sydney

Library of Congress Cataloging-in-Publication Data
Sanford, William R. (William Reynolds), 1927–
    Sandy Koufax / by William R. Sanford and Carl R. Green. — 1st ed.
        p.   cm. — (Sports immortals)
    Includes bibliographical references.
    ISBN 0-89686-780-3
    1. Koufax, Sandy, 1935–   —Juvenile literature. 2. Baseball players—United States—Biography—Juvenile literature.
3. Los Angeles Dodgers (Baseball team)—History—Juvenile literature. I. Green, Carl R.   II. Title.   III. Series.
GV865.K67S26   1993
796.357'092—dc20
[B]   92-31249

Photo Credits
All photos courtesy of AP—Wide World Photos.

CRESTWOOD HOUSE

Macmillan Publishing Company
866 Third Avenue
New York, NY 10022

Maxwell Macmillan Canada, Inc.
1200 Eglinton Avenue East
Suite 200
Don Mills, Ontario M3C 3N1

Macmillan Publishing Company is part of the Maxwell Communication Group of Companies.

Produced by Flying Fish Studio

Printed in the United States of America

First edition

10 9 8 7 6 5 4 3 2 1

CONTENTS

Sandy Koufax, a legend on the pitcher's mound

4

THE PERFECT GAME

September 9, 1965, was a big night for the Los Angeles Dodgers. At Dodger Stadium 29,139 fans waited tensely for the first pitch. The home team, half a game behind the San Francisco Giants, was facing the Chicago Cubs. Manager Walt Alston named Sandy Koufax as his starting pitcher.

Despite a three-game losing streak, the ace lefty had not been pitching badly. Dodger batters simply hadn't been scoring enough runs. But Sandy knew his 21–7 record would not mean much if the team lost the **pennant**. Dodger fans were also worried about their star's left elbow. Sandy had been pitching in pain all year.

Warming up before the game, Sandy said his elbow felt fine. In the first inning, however, he realized that his fastball was only average. In his younger days Sandy might have blown the ball sky high. Now he turned to his sharp-breaking curve to baffle the Cub batters. Bob Hendley, the Cub pitcher, matched him pitch for pitch. After four innings the scoreboard showed only goose eggs: no hits, no runs, no errors.

The Dodgers broke the tie in the bottom of the fifth. Left fielder Lou Johnson walked and was bunted to second. When Johnson tried to steal third, the Cub catcher threw wildly. The error allowed Sweet Lou to score. The Dodgers still were hitless, but they had scratched out a run.

Sandy prepares to flash a fastball past a Chicago Cub, en route to a perfect pitching game.

With two outs in the top of the seventh, .315-hitting Billy Williams walked to the plate. Pitching too carefully, Sandy threw three straight balls. Rather than give up a walk, he fired a strike down the center of the plate. With the count 3–1, Williams swung hard—and flied out. In the bottom of the inning, Johnson tagged Hendley for a bloop double to right. The base hit was the Dodgers' first (and only) hit of the game.

In the eighth the heart of the Cubs' lineup struck out, one-two-three. Sandy's fastball had come to life. The first two batters in the ninth went down the same way. That brought Harvey Kuenn to the plate. A .303 lifetime hitter, Kuenn had struck out only 16 times that year. But this was Sandy's night. Kuenn went down swinging on three blazing fastballs.

Sandy walked off the mound with his fourth no-hitter and first perfect game. Twenty-seven Cubs had come to the plate. None of them had reached first base. The kid from Brooklyn had earned himself a place among baseball's immortals.

GROWING UP IN BROOKLYN

Sanford "Sandy" Koufax began life on December 30, 1935. At that time his parents, Evelyn and Jack Braun, were living in the Borough Park section of Brooklyn. When Sandy was three, Evelyn divorced her husband and moved in with her parents. Grandmother and Grandfather Lichtenstein took care of Sandy while Evelyn was at work. The Jewish household observed all of their religious holidays.

When he was old enough, Sandy played a game called stoopball. In this game one player throws a hard rubber ball against some apartment house steps (the "stoop"). A second player tries to catch the ball before it hits the ground. Sandy's favorite ball was the Spalding (the kids called it a Spal-deen).

Even at age eight, Sandy had the makings of a future baseball star.

Stoopball soon gave way to a team game called punchball. Instead of a bat, punchball players hit the Spal-deen with their fists. From there Sandy moved up to stickball, played with a tennis ball and a broom handle. Fire hydrants and parked cars served as bases.

Evelyn married a lawyer named Irving Koufax when Sandy was nine. In later years Sandy always spoke of Irving as his father. The marriage also gave him a sister, Irving's daughter Edith. Soon after the wedding the family moved to Rockville Centre on Long Island. The local high school, with its sports fields, lay across the street.

Sandy spent every free moment outdoors. He played football during the fall and baseball all summer. In those days youth leagues did not exist. The boys played pickup games with their own rules. Strangely enough, Sandy played every position on these kid teams except one. He does not remember being asked to pitch.

For his tenth birthday Sandy's grandparents gave him a Rollfast bicycle. Riding the maroon bike almost ended his athletic career before it began. Sandy pedaled into the street one day and was hit by a car. He had to sit out the football season while he waited for his knee to heal.

The Koufaxes moved back to Brooklyn on the day Sandy graduated from ninth grade. Basketball was the favorite playground game there. Sandy threw himself into the sport and earned a spot on the Jewish Community House squad. The team went on to win the Jewish Welfare Board national championship.

Sandy played baseball for the Tomahawks in the summer Ice Cream League. He wore borrowed spikes because Irving refused to buy him a new pair. That was before the lawyer saw Sandy pitch. After watching his son strike out the side, Irving ran to a pay phone and called Evelyn. "What's the idea of letting that kid play with old shoes?" he demanded. "You want him to hurt himself?" When Sandy took the field for the next game, he was wearing new spikes. The Tomahawks won the league championship that year, 1952.

At Lafayette High School, Sandy emerged as a basketball star. He had grown to six feet, two inches, and he was a fine jumper. During his senior year he was chosen as team captain and made the all-city team. Sandy also played for the Lafayette baseball team—as a weak-hitting first baseman. A coach for the Coney Island Parkviews talked him into working harder on his pitching. Sandy gave up plenty of walks, but when his fastball was on target, it overpowered the hitters. Baseball **scouts** began to show up at games he was scheduled to pitch. Sandy did not worry about impressing them. Basketball was still his first love.

 Although Sandy went on to become a baseball immortal, at one time he thought his future lay in playing basketball. Did he have a chance of making it in the National Basketball League?

* Answers to all Trivia Quiz questions can be found on pages 46–47.

THE SCOUTS COME CALLING

As his June 1953 graduation neared, Sandy looked at his options. If he wanted to train to be an architect, he'd have to go to college. His grades, however, were only a little above average. He thought a basketball scholarship was his best bet.

A recruiter for the University of Cincinnati invited Sandy for a tryout. The school's coaches liked his style and awarded him a scholarship. When the fall term began, Sandy enrolled as a liberal arts major. He told himself he would later transfer to the school of architecture.

The freshman team was thrown into practice against the Bearcat varsity. Sandy held his own against Jack Twyman, who later starred in pro basketball. Under coach Ed Jucker, the freshmen won 12 games and lost only 2. Sandy emerged as a key rebounder and the team's third best scorer. A 23-point effort against Miami of Ohio marked his season high.

When basketball ended, Jucker put on his second cap, that of varsity baseball coach. Hanging around the coach's office one day, Sandy heard the magic words "spring trip." He learned that the baseball team was about to leave for New Orleans. "Coach, take me along," Sandy said. "I'm a baseball player. I'm a pitcher."

TRIVIA 2

After Sandy pitched his first no-hitter for the Coney Island Parkviews, he showed the game ball to his parents. How did his father react?

Eighteen-year-old Sandy in his University of Cincinnati baseball uniform

Jucker soon saw why **major league** scouts were interested. This boy could throw *hard!* On the trip south he pitched Sandy against an air force team. Sandy's lack of experience showed. The team's minor leaguers knocked him out of the box in the fifth inning. Back in Ohio, Sandy settled down and pitched a four-hitter. In his next start he set a school record with 18 Ks (strikeouts) and beat Louisville. Sandy finished the season with a 3–1 record. He rang up 51 strikeouts in 31 innings, but also gave up 30 walks.

Bill Zinser, a scout for the Brooklyn Dodgers, took Sandy aside. Zinser offered him a trip to Brooklyn to work out at Ebbets Field. Sandy told the scout that he lived in Brooklyn. "You can get in touch with me any time during the summer," he said. Sandy also talked to scouts from the New York Giants and the Pittsburgh Pirates.

Back home, the Giants invited Sandy to a tryout. When he reached the Polo Grounds, he had to borrow a glove and a uniform. Then he walked onto a big league field for the first time. With his nerves in tatters, Sandy's fastballs hit everything but the catcher's mitt. The Giants quickly crossed him off their list.

A Pittsburgh scout watched Sandy strike out 15 batters in a summer league game. He was shelled in his next game, but the Pirates invited him to a tryout anyway. This time Sandy conquered his nervousness and pitched well. The Pirates wanted to sign him, but the front office was having money problems. By the time the team put an offer together, it was too late.

Late that summer, Sandy went to Ebbets Field for a workout with his hometown team. Sandy threw fastballs for the better part of an hour. Al Campanis, the chief scout, said later, "I actually had trouble seeing the ball at times."

Buzzie Bavasi, the Dodger general manager, made up his mind. "Sign him," he told Campanis.

TRIVIA 3

Dodger catcher John Roseboro once buzzed a throw just past Juan Marichal's ear. Enraged, the Giant pitcher hit Roseboro with his bat. Why did teammates say later that the whole affair happened because Sandy was the Dodger pitcher that day?

ThE BOnUS BABy, 1955-1957

When contract talks began, Irving acted as Sandy's agent. He told the Dodgers that his son wanted a $20,000 bonus. The money, he reasoned, would pay for college if Sandy failed as a ball player.

The Dodgers agreed, but said that $6,000 of the $20,000 had to count as Sandy's first-year salary. Irving and Dodger owner Walter O'Malley shook hands on the deal. That handshake cost Sandy at least $10,000. The Milwaukee Braves jumped into the bidding that fall with an offer of $30,000.

In 1954 any club that paid a large bonus like the one that Sandy was paid had to keep the **rookie** on its **roster** for at least two years. The rule (later dropped) was passed to keep the rich clubs from signing all the best prospects. No one worried much about its effect on the **bonus babies**. Young men like Sandy were no longer given time to learn their trade in the **minor leagues**.

Sandy drove to Florida in February 1955 to begin his career as a Dodger. The Vero Beach **spring training** camp had once been a navy base. The buildings were shabby, gray relics of World War II. Sandy shared a tiny room with a teammate. The shower was down the hall. When workouts started, a locker room attendant handed Sandy uniform number 32.

Sandy dressed beside Pee Wee Reese, Jackie Robinson, Gil Hodges, and the other Dodger stars. Out on the field he joined his fellow pitchers for workouts. His first task, he learned, was to run and run, and run some more to get in shape. When he started throwing, he quickly developed a sore arm. Throw through the soreness, Sandy was told. Then go run some more laps.

13

The Dodgers left Florida with a 25-man roster. To clear a spot for Sandy, the Dodgers released Tommy Lasorda, who later returned as their manager. When the season opened, the team jumped off to a fast start, except for Sandy. Game after game, he sat on the bench and watched his teammates play.

On June 24 manager Walter Alston put Sandy into a game the Dodgers were losing 7–1. Wild and nervous, Sandy loaded the bases before striking out Bobby Thomson. A double play ended the inning, and he breezed through the ninth. After pitching an inning against the Giants, Sandy made his first start, on July 6. He lasted into the fifth, giving up eight walks and only three hits. His next start did not come until August 27. This time Sandy showed the stuff that the Dodgers had been waiting to see. He shut out Cincinnati on two hits and struck out 14 batters.

The Cincinnati **shutout** was the high point of 1955 for Sandy. His record for the year: two wins, two losses. In slightly over 40 innings he gave up 28 walks and 33 hits. Alston looked at those numbers and kept him on the bench during the World Series. Behind Johnny Podres, the team beat the Yankees in seven games.

The Dodgers sent Sandy to Puerto Rico to pitch in a winter league. Playing winter ball did not cure his wildness. Still fighting his control, Sandy appeared in only 16 games in 1956, with two wins and four losses. Given ten starts, he was knocked out of the box in nine of them. No longer a bonus baby in 1957, he managed to hang on as a big leaguer. That year he appeared in 34 games, winning five and losing four. After three full seasons his record showed only nine wins against ten losses.

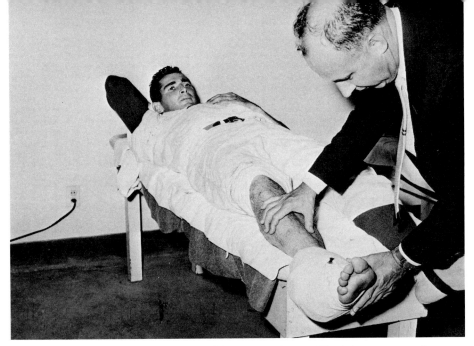

Sandy's injured ankle is examined by a team doctor. The injury occurred when Sandy, running to cover first base, collided with a Cubs runner.

THE LEARNING YEARS, 1958-1960

The third-place Dodgers ended the 1957 season in Philadelphia. Sandy finished the game by striking out the final Philly batter. It was the last pitch thrown by a Brooklyn Dodger. In 1958 the team moved to the West Coast.

Team owner Walter O'Malley saw Los Angeles as an untapped market for big league baseball. With the city's help he began building a stadium in Chavez Ravine, just north of downtown. While they waited for their new home, the Dodgers played in the Memorial Coliseum. When the huge football stadium was set up for baseball, it seated 93,000. The left field fence, guarded by a high screen, lay only 250 feet from home plate. Sandy worried that fly balls hit to left would turn into cheap home runs. By contrast, the right field fence, at 440 feet, seemed a mile away.

15

The move seemed to agree with Sandy at first. On July 1 his record stood at an eye-opening 7–3. Then he went into a tailspin along with his team. The Dodgers finished in seventh place, and Sandy ended with an 11–11 record. His 131 strikeouts were balanced by 105 walks and 17 wild pitches.

Sandy's baseball future looked even bleaker in 1959. Opposing batters knocked him out of the box in five of his first six starts. The Dodgers came close to giving up on him. Pitching coach Joe Becker reported, "He has no coordination and he has lost all his confidence." Sandy felt his best hope was that some other team would pick him up.

Then, in mid-June, the magic returned. Sandy pitched three straight complete games and set his first strikeout records. He followed a 13-strikeout game with 18 Ks against the San Francisco Giants. The 18 strikeouts tied a major league record. A week later, after whiffing ten Cubs, Sandy owned the three-game strikeout record. The old record had belonged to Hall of Famers Walter Johnson and Bob Feller.

Sandy wears a big smile after a superb pitching performance that led the Dodgers to a 6–2 win over the Philadelphia Phillies.

The Dodgers fought their way into the World Series against the Chicago White Sox. In the first game, with the Dodgers behind 11–0, Sandy made his Series debut. He made the most of his chance by turning in two perfect innings of relief. After that sharp effort, Alston named Sandy as his starter in game five. Sandy pitched well, but the White Sox hurler pitched better. A Coliseum crowd of 92,706 groaned as the Dodgers lost a tight 1–0 game. The pain of the loss was eased in game six. Old pro Johnny Podres beat the White Sox 9–3 to give Los Angeles its first championship.

The promise Sandy displayed in 1959 seemed to fade in 1960. At season's end his record showed only 8 wins against 13 losses. On the plus side, he was learning his craft. An improved curve and a change-up made his fastball more effective. What he hadn't learned was a cure for his streaks of wildness.

By then Sandy had decided to make his home in California. He bought a house and invested in a business. His poor 1960 season made Sandy think about quitting baseball. With no wife or family to support, he was free to do what he wanted. What he wanted to do, he decided, was play baseball. Sandy sold his business and devoted himself to preparing for the 1961 season.

TRIVIA 4

Twice during his career Sandy struck out 18 batters in a nine-inning game. That mark was eclipsed in 1986 by a fireballing right-hander. Who is the pitcher and how many batters did he strike out?

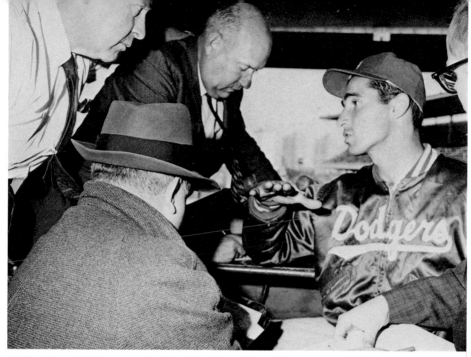

Following a 1961 game, Sandy talks about his strikeout powers with reporters.

A STAR EMERGES, 1961-1962

In the spring of 1961, Dodger statistician Allan Roth showed Sandy some useful facts. When he was ahead in the count, batters hit only .146 against him. When he was behind, their average jumped to .267. Clearly, the first pitch was the key. Once he had the count his way, hitters had to go after his pitch. Okay, Sandy thought. How do I get that first pitch over the plate?

The answer to that question turned Sandy into a great pitcher. First, his coaches advised him to take a smaller, tighter **windup**. When you rear back in that big windup, they said, you lose sight of your target. Next, catcher Norm Sherry added a second bit of advice. Sherry told Sandy he was less effective when he tried to overpower every batter. "You don't have to throw that hard," he said.

Sandy began throwing with a loose, easy motion. To his surprise, his speed improved along with his control. The new motion hid his pitches better, too. Old habits die hard, however. When Sandy was in a tight spot, he sometimes tried to blow one past a batter. That was when Sherry would walk out to the mound. "Be a pitcher," he would say. "Make them swing the bat and maybe you'll get out of the inning."

Between mid-May and mid-June, Sandy ran up a six-game winning streak. By July his 10–3 record earned him a place on the National League All-Star team. Sandy began to dream of a 20-win season. As it turned out, he won only eight more games that year. Still, that was seven more games than he had ever won before. Further, his 269 Ks broke the National League strikeout mark.

It took a great deal of coordination and concentration for Sandy to obtain the control that he needed for his fast pitches.

In 1962 the Dodgers moved into their new stadium at Chavez Ravine. For Sandy, it was an up-and-down season. On the plus side were games that featured his first no-hitter and an 18-strikeout effort. His 2.54 **earned run average (ERA)** led the National League. But he also had to cope with his first serious injury.

In May the index finger of his pitching hand turned numb. Trainers told him that loss of circulation is common among pitchers. Luckily, he used the index finger only to grip the ball. Sandy's fastball and curve continued to spin off his middle finger. Pitching despite the numbness, he struck out 49 batters in his next four games. For the first time he finished a game without giving up a walk. And, wonder of wonders, he hit a home run off the great Warren Spahn. The no-hitter came in June against the bumbling New York Mets.

In early July a specialist diagnosed the index finger problem as a loss of blood flow. No one was certain that the condition could be cured. At that point Sandy's record was a sparkling 14–4. Tests showed the finger was receiving only 15 percent of its normal blood supply. A treatment plan using four different medicines finally cured the problem. Doctors told Sandy he had been close to losing the finger.

TRIVIA
5

Only three players have repeated as MVPs in the World Series. Sandy was World Series MVP in 1963 and 1965. Who are the other two?

Sandy is surrounded by jubilant teammates after his no-hitter game brought the Dodgers to a 5–0 victory over the New York Mets in June 1962.

Number 32 returned to the pitching mound in late September. Out of shape after his close call, Sandy did not win another game that year. The first-place Dodgers also hit a losing streak. The team fell into a tie with the Giants and lost the pennant in a three-game play-off. The Dodgers went home, and the Giants went to the World Series.

The windup and delivery of another perfect pitch

YEARS OF GREATNESS, 1963-1964

For a quiet, somewhat shy man like Sandy, 1963 was both a trial and a triumph. All through the winter he heard the same question time after time: "How's the finger?" As his record would soon prove, the finger was fine. Blood flow was up to 85 percent of normal.

The Dodgers gave Sandy a raise to $35,000 a year. He joined Duke Snider, Don Drysdale and other Dodgers in Milton Berle's nightclub act. The Las Vegas audiences loved it when Berle asked Sandy, "How's the finger?"

"It's great," Sandy would reply. After a pause he would add, "All I've got now is a little problem with my thumb." Then he would hold up a huge fake thumb. The skit always earned a big laugh.

Sandy opened the season with a five-hitter against the Cubs. Then the injury jinx popped up again. In mid-April a sore shoulder put him out of action for two weeks. He came back strong, and by mid-May he was 6–1. On May 11, pitching against the hated Giants, he chalked up his second no-hitter. By mid-July the Dodger star was an incredible 17–3. That was the month he threw three shutouts in a row and played in his second All-Star game. For an encore he pitched the Dodgers into the World Series against the New York Yankees.

The Yankee scouting report said of Sandy, "Simply the best." The Dodger lefty's numbers proved the point. Sandy ended the year with a 25–5 record, including 11 shutouts. His ERA of 1.88 was the lowest in the National League in 20 years. Most amazing of all, in 311 innings Sandy walked only 58 batters. The former wild man was now a control pitcher!

Sandy prepares to fire a strike past a Yankee batter during an early inning of this 1963 World Series game.

23

Sandy jumps for joy after pitching the Dodgers to a 2–1 victory over the New York Yankees in the fourth and final game of the 1963 World Series.

The 1963 Yankees were a pitcher's nightmare. Dodger pitchers, however, kept Mickey Mantle, Roger Maris, and the other Bronx Bombers under control. Sandy pitched a brilliant first game, striking out 15 Yankees to break a World Series record. The Dodgers won 5–2 and never looked back. Sandy returned to win the fourth and final game 2–1. Once again the Dodgers were world champions. Sandy was named Most Valuable Player for the 1963 season and won his first Cy Young Award.

Sandy paid a stiff price for pitching those 311 innings. The human arm is not designed for throwing baseballs 90-plus mph. Curveballs put an extra strain on the shoulder, elbow, and wrist. During the winter scar tissue would form where the muscles had been torn. When spring training began each year, Sandy had to break down these **adhesions**. That meant a week or two of pain and internal bleeding.

In 1964 Sandy's adhesions refused to break loose. He started slowly, building an early-season record of 4–4. With Joe Becker's help he fixed a flaw in his delivery. After that he roared back to win 15 of his next 16 games. On August 8, with his record 19–5, Sandy hurt his elbow diving into second base. The swelling and soreness lasted for days but felt better after he warmed up. On August 17 the injury caught up with him. Sandy woke to find his left arm swollen from the wrist to the shoulder.

X rays showed traumatic **arthritis**. The team doctor drained the arm and gave Sandy a cortisone shot. Two weeks later Sandy tried to warm up, but the swelling returned. By then the Dodgers had fallen out of the pennant race. The Dodger brain trust told Sandy to rest his arm until spring training.

Sandy holds up three fingers to denote the third no-hit game of his career.

25

During spring training, Sandy warms up his arthritic elbow.

PITCHING IN PAIN, 1965-1966

Sandy's left arm held center stage when spring training opened in 1965. At first the arm seemed fine, but then it swelled up again. After each game trainers iced his arm to keep down the swelling. Sandy found that he could live with the pain.

Taking the mound in the season's fourth game, Sandy looked like the Koufax of old. Batters wondered if he really had a sore arm. His sharp pitching earned him a start in the All-Star game. On July 20 Sandy ran his record to 17–3 with his eleventh straight win. That set the stage for September. Sandy capped a near-perfect season by throwing a perfect game against the Cubs.

Sandy carried a 26–8 record into the World Series against the Minnesota Twins. But game one was scheduled on the Jewish holiday of Yom Kippur. As he had all through his career, Sandy refused to pitch on the high holy days.

Drysdale lost the first game and Sandy lost the second. Down 2–0, the Dodgers rallied to even the Series. Sandy came back strong in the fifth game and put his team on top with a four-hitter. The never-say-die Twins won game six. That left it up to Sandy in game seven. Pitching on two days' rest, he threw a three-hitter to wrap up the Series. In the weeks that followed, Sandy won his second Cy Young Award and his second Hickok Belt. The Cy

TRIVIA 6 Sandy still holds the record for the most strikeouts in a four-game World Series. How many Yankees did he strike out in the 1963 series?

Despite the fact that he was suffering from pain throughout most of the year, 1965 was an award-winning season for Sandy.

Young goes to the league's best pitcher. The Hickok is awarded to the Professional Athlete of the Year.

That winter Sandy joined Don Drysdale in **holding out** for a big raise. General manager Buzzie Bavasi did not feel much pressure. Because they belonged to the Dodgers, the players could not jump to another team. To force the issue, the two stars said they would refuse to report to spring training.

Rumors said that each man wanted $500,000 for three years. Sports pages ran headlines asking, "Holdout or Holdup?" The Dodgers countered by offering Sandy a one-year contract for $100,000. Only the great Willie Mays commanded a higher salary. The contract war dragged on until late March, when both sides gave a little. Sandy signed for $125,000, baseball's top salary at the time. His income increased even more when Viking Press paid him $110,000 to write his life story.

Few pitchers could throw the ball as hard or as fast as Sandy Koufax.

Some players take it easy after winning a big contract. Not Sandy. His arm still hurt, but he pitched a workhorse 323 innings in 1966. He struck out 16 Phillies in a July game and notched his twentieth win on August 21. On the last day of the season, the Dodgers were playing a doubleheader with Houston. Needing the second game to stay in first, Alston asked Sandy to pitch on two days' rest. The Dodger ace responded by blanking the Astros for eight innings. He weakened in the ninth, but held on to win 6–3. Los Angeles sportswriters looked at his 27–9 record and called him "Goldfinger." The sterling season also earned him a third Cy Young Award.

Worn out by the pennant race, the Dodgers lost the series to Baltimore in four games. Sandy took the loss in the second game. Less than a month later, he called a press conference. The news that came out of that meeting shocked the sports world.

A slew of reporters were on hand for the press conference in which Sandy announced his retirement from baseball.

THE BOMBSHELL

Sports news seldom finds room on page one. That rule was broken on November 18, 1966. The headline in the *New York Times* summed up the bombshell news:

KOUFAX, DODGER PITCHING STAR,
RETIRES BECAUSE OF AILING ARM

Never before had a pitcher retired at the top of his career, but Sandy always had been one of a kind. The 30-year-old star announced his retirement at a press conference.

"I have asked the Dodgers to put me on the voluntary retired list," he said. "A few too many shots . . . a few too many pills," he explained. "I could be doing this a year too soon, but that's the way it is. I don't want to take a chance of completely disabling myself and losing the use of my left arm. It didn't get any better last year and it is worse this fall than last fall."

The Dodgers had been dreading the news. When the 1966 season ended, Sandy told Bavasi that it was likely his last. The pain in his elbow was getting worse. The pills, shots, and therapy did not help much. Most alarming of all, Sandy found that he could not fully straighten his arm. More and more, he was teaching himself to do everyday tasks with his right hand.

Reports said that the Dodgers had offered Sandy $150,000 to pitch at least one more year. Sandy knew that was a generous offer, but he turned it down. Money would not buy a new arm. He did not want to end up a bitter, crippled old ballplayer.

Dr. Robert Kerlan said that Sandy had fallen victim to arthritis. Every curveball he threw wrenched the elbow. The injury he suffered sliding into second base in 1964 had made the problem worse. Kerlan added that he did not think the arthritis would spread. Out of baseball, Sandy could enjoy a long and healthy life. He could still play golf and other sports that did not demand throwing.

A reporter asked Sandy if the Dodgers might keep him as a hitter. That question drew a big laugh. Most pitchers are poor hitters, and Sandy was one of the worst. His lifetime **batting average** was a puny .097. Sandy went on to say that he did not want to act or go into politics. He said he was going on vacation in the Bahamas. Afterward, he would think about his future.

TRIVIA 7 | Walter Johnson holds the major league record for shutouts with 110, but it took him 21 years to reach that total. How many shutouts did Sandy rack up in his 12-year career?

The love and support of friends and fans were helpful to Sandy during his difficult decision to retire.

Tributes poured in from across the baseball world. Leo Durocher, no mean judge of talent, called Sandy "the best pitcher I've ever seen." Red Sox general manager Dick O'Connell added his own praise. "Sandy Koufax has to rank with the great pitchers in the history of the game," he said.

An editorial in the *New York Times* honored the Brooklyn boy. "Remember," the paper said, "that he retired with honor and dignity instead of negotiating a huge 1967 contract and then quitting after a few games. . . . Remember him as a gentle, quiet man but a fierce competitor who winced with arthritic pain with almost every pitch in the last few years. . . . He has retired from the diamond; but he will be long remembered as a great player and a great human being."

TRIVIA 8 Opposing batters never had much luck against Sandy's overpowering "stuff." What was their combined batting average during the 12 years he pitched for the Dodgers?

THE RETIREMENT YEARS

Looking back to his early retirement, Sandy shakes his head a little sadly. "I had a bunch of spurs in [my elbow]," he says. "Today I could have had surgery over the winter and been back the next season."

As he nears his sixtieth birthday, Sandy still looks like a world-class athlete. Tanned and fit, he keeps his weight down with golf, jogging, and a busy schedule. Even though he has been retired for over 25 years, fans still ask for his autograph. When he appears in public, women run up and put their arms around him. Sandy tries to smile as their husbands snap a picture or two.

After walking away from the Dodgers, Sandy looked once more at his options. Some of his fans thought he might return to college to study architecture. The lure of staying close to sports proved greater. Sandy signed a ten-year contract with NBC to do color and interviews for the Game of the Week. Still shy after 12 years in the spotlight, Sandy was not cut out to be a broadcaster. He stuck with the job for six years and then quit.

Koufax fans were happy to tune in and see their pitching hero as a broadcaster for NBC Sports.

33

Sandy and his bride, the former Anne Heath Widmark, gaze fondly at each other during their 1969 marriage ceremony.

For years magazines had called Sandy one of the nation's most eligible bachelors. In 1969 he gave up his single life and married Anne Heath Widmark. The wedding took place in the West Hollywood home of the bride's father, actor Richard Widmark. The couple set up housekeeping in an old farmhouse near East Holden, Maine. Sandy joked that he was swapping his golf shoes for snowshoes.

The spotlight pursued Sandy even as he sought a quiet life with his books and music. In January 1972 sportswriters elected him to baseball's Hall of Fame. The 344 votes he received were the highest total in 40 years of voting. At age 36, Sandy set another record as well. He was the youngest player ever elected to the Hall of Fame.

This plaque shows Sandy as a 1972 inductee into the Baseball Hall of Fame.

Sandy welcomed the honor. "For anyone who has played professional baseball, it's the greatest honor that can come to you," he said. He added that he had not been certain he would be picked. "Election to the Hall is a recognition of a long career of excellence, and I felt that my career might be too short."

Not to be outdone, the Dodgers retired his number 32 that same year. In 1979 the team lured Sandy back to the game as a part-time pitching coach. To begin the year, he travels to Vero Beach to work with Dodger pitchers. During the season he visits the team's farm clubs. Rookies who weren't born when Sandy was setting strikeout records hang on his every word. Crowds gather when he throws batting practice.

Maine's long, cold winters drove the Koufaxes back to California. For a while they lived in a small town in central California. In 1984 they moved again, this time to Santa Barbara. Wherever Sandy lives, his neighbors learn to guard his privacy. Fans can still see him in **old-timers' games**, however. Baseball is in his blood.

Asked why he took the coaching job with the Dodgers, Sandy counted off the reasons. "It was hard to stay away from the one thing I had done well in my life," he said. "I needed a job. I enjoy working with kids." Then he added the clincher. "It's fun."

TRIVIA 9 — Sandy holds a share of the Dodger record for striking out the most batters in a single inning. What is the record?

The 1985 All-Star National League team chose Sandy as the honorary captain. Here he pitches to his team during batting practice.

Sandy will be remembered as one of the greatest pitchers in the history of baseball.

SANDY KOUFAX, BASEBALL IMMORTAL

In 1963 teammate Tommy Davis hugged Sandy after he closed out the Yankees in the World Series. "Sandy, you are the greatest pitcher that ever lived!" Davis told him.

Sandy's 1963 numbers had earned that kind of praise. His 25-5 record led the league, as did his 1.88 ERA. His 306 strikeouts broke his own National League record. Among his honors that year were the Cy Young Award and the National League's MVP.

The idea of being called "the greatest" did not sit well with Sandy. "Let me be around a while," he said later to reporters. "Sure I've had a great year, and I'm proud of it. But before you talk about me in the same class with the great ones, let me prove I can win for many years, not one."

Sandy holds the Cy Young Award, naming him as best pitcher of 1966.

Fans are shown climbing on the Dodger dugout roof trying to get an autograph from Sandy as he leaves the field.

Sandy's arthritic elbow ended his career after only 12 years. Six of those years he spent learning to control his 93.2 mph fastball. Only in the last six years did he win Cy Young awards and set records. For five years in a row his ERA was the best in the league. His four no-hitters led all of baseball until Nolan Ryan chalked up numbers five, six, and seven. In 1973 Ryan also erased Sandy's single-season strikeout mark, 383 to 382.

TRIVIA 10

When Sandy retired after the 1966 season, many baseball experts predicted that without him the Dodgers would nosedive in the standings. Were the predictions correct?

Some of Sandy's key numbers did not make the record books. He is the only National League pitcher to twice strike out the side on nine pitches. Over his career he averaged more than one strikeout per inning pitched. That type of pitching made the Dodger defense stronger. If Sandy struck out 15 Reds, the fielders had to handle only 12 more chances. Because he usually threw complete games, the bullpen could count on an easy night when Sandy was starting. The hitters also felt less pressure. Knowing that Sandy would give up only a run or two, they could scratch for two or three.

Members of the 1962 Dodger pitching staff (left to right)*: Don Drysdale, Pete Richert, Stan Williams, Sandy Koufax and Johnny Podres.*

Some of Sandy's greatest tributes came from opposing batters. The New York Mets were winless against Sandy when they beat him in mid-season 1965. Overjoyed, the Mets cheered as if they had just won the pennant. Pittsburgh's Willie Stargell spoke for his fellow hitters when he described what it felt like to hit against the great lefty. "Trying to hit Sandy Koufax," he said, "was like trying to drink coffee with a fork."

Sandy's outstanding pitching earned him the right to be classified as a sports immortal.

GLOSSARY

adhesion—A condition in which muscle fibers are stuck together by scar tissue. The adhesions keep the muscles from stretching and contracting normally.

arthritis—A painful inflammation of the joints. Arthritis can be caused by injury, overwork, or the natural process of aging.

batting average—A measure of a batter's success at the plate. A hitter's batting average is figured by dividing the number of hits by the times at bat. Thus, Sandy Koufax's 75 hits in 776 times at bat gave him a lifetime batting average of .097.

bonus baby—Under the old bonus rule, a team that signed a rookie for a large bonus was forced to keep the youngster on its big league roster for at least two years.

earned run average (ERA)—A measure of a pitcher's success in keeping the opposing team from scoring. Earned run averages are calculated by figuring the number of earned runs allowed per each nine innings pitched. When Sandy pitched 223 innings in 1964 and gave up only 43 earned runs, he was credited with an ERA of 1.74.

holdouts—Ballplayers who refuse to report for spring training until the team pays them the salaries they think they deserve.

major leagues—The highest level of organized baseball. Only teams belonging to the American and National leagues can currently be called major league.

minor leagues—The lower levels of organized baseball. Most players begin their careers in the minors, hoping to work their way up to the majors.

oldtimers' game—An exhibition game played by retired major league stars.

pennant—A team that "wins a pennant" has won its league championship. Pennant winners go on to play in the World Series.

rookie—A ballplayer who is playing in the major leagues for the first time.

roster—The list of players who are eligible to play for a team. League rules set the number of players who can be carried on a team's roster.

scout—Someone hired to observe young ballplayers to see if they have the talent needed to play professional baseball.

shutout—A game in which a pitcher prevents the opposing team from scoring.

spring training—The weeks during the spring that baseball teams set aside to prepare their players for the coming season.

windup—The motions a pitcher goes through before throwing each pitch.

MORE GOOD READING ABOUT SANDY KOUFAX

Grabowski, John. *Sandy Koufax.* New York: Chelsea House Publishers, 1992.

Hano, Arnold. *Sandy Koufax, Strikeout King.* New York: G. P. Putnam's Sons, 1966.

Koufax, Sandy (with Ed Linn). *Koufax.* New York: Viking Press, 1966.

Mitchell, Jerry. *Sandy Koufax.* New York: Grosset & Dunlap, 1966.

Sullivan, Neil J. *The Dodgers Move West.* New York: Oxford University Press, 1987.

Whittingham, Richard. *The Los Angeles Dodgers: An Illustrated History.* New York: Harper & Row, 1982.

SANDY KOUFAX TRIVIA QUIZ

1: According to Harry Gallatin, who starred for the New York Knicks in the 1950s, the answer was "Yes!" After scrimmaging against Sandy's Lafayette High School team, Gallatin said, "[Sandy] has a real future in pro basketball. He's got a tremendous leap and for such a big kid, he moves like a cat." During Sandy's senior year many of the big basketball schools offered him athletic scholarships. He chose Cincinnati because of its good school of architecture.

2: At that time Irving Koufax had never seen Sandy pitch. When told of the no-hitter, he joked with Sandy and teased him about the other team's hitting ability.

3: Dodger hitters were convinced that Marichal had been throwing at them. Normally, when an opposing pitcher throws too close to your batters, you expect your own pitcher to retaliate. Roseboro, knowing that Sandy never knocked batters down on purpose, took matters into his own hands.

4: Roger Clemens of the Boston Red Sox struck out 20 opposing hitters in his record-setting game.

5: Sandy was the first to win two World Series MVP awards. He has since been joined by Bob Gibson (1964 and 1967) and Reggie Jackson (1973 and 1977).

6: Sandy struck out 23 Yankee batters during the 1963 series. Bob Gibson of the St. Louis Cardinals holds the record for a seven-game series with 35. Gibson also broke Sandy's single-game record of 15 when he struck out 17 in 1968.

7: Sandy was credited with 40 shutouts during his 12-year career. Thirty-one of them came during his last four years. If he could have continued that pace for ten more years, he would have shattered Johnson's record.

8: National League hitters collected only 1,754 hits in 8,578 times at bat against Sandy. That works out to a combined batting average of .204.

9: Twice during his career Sandy struck out four batters in a single inning. This unusual event occurs when a batter strikes out on a wild pitch or a passed ball. The pitcher receives credit for a strikeout even though the batter makes it safely to first base.

10: Yes, the experts were right for once. After winning the National League pennant in 1966, the Koufax-less Dodgers fell all the way to eighth place.

index